The Humour of Hard Hitting Reality

Arsham Hirani

Printed in India

IndiePress

ISBN: 978-93-6045-973-4

First Printing, 2024

Indie Press

A division of Nasadiya Technologies Private Ltd.

Koramangala, Bengaluru

Karnataka-560029

http://indiepress.in/

Contents

SOME HUMOROUS PARTS
OF MY CHILDHOOD

Arsham Hirani

My extremely fruitful morning in a page

Call me lazy, idle, sluggish, sleepyhead,
Or invent another disgraceful term
From that expansive dictionary of derogatory slander.
My apologies! But I am simply not your morning person,
Not the early bird whose rising is synchronous with the sun,
Nor the one who nearly breaks his bones
While failing to replicate bewildering yoga poses,
Nor the punctual one who tucks his bedsheet,
Nor the one interested in gazing at austere skies.

Instead, the one whose deep slumber remains unaltered
Despite several blaring alarms, while at the door,
Mother pounds, then succeeds in her arduous task.
Her threat of a bucket of ice-cold water jolts me out of bed.
Getting dressed, brushing - and the monotonous old drill.
Indecisiveness in hair styling wastes precious moments,
Then scrambling and panicking to search for my tie,
Only to find it tossed away in some sordid corner.

Alarmed that merely five minutes are pending
Until the bus arrives outside my abode,
I guzzle a glass of milk, scarcely eating the scrambled egg,
Infuriating the cook for his industriousness.
With a rasher of bread smeared with jam in hand,
I rush towards the stop at lightning speed
To catch the bus before it leaves.

While fortunately, there it lies waiting,
Thanks to my slightly more punctual sibling,
Who assures the driver the delay shall not be prolonged.
As I enter, his threats and reproaches fall on my deaf ears
Now that's what I call a true student.

Kids pushing themselves outside their comfort zone

Well, Indian train journeys, I felt, were a suicide mission.
The Odisha rail crash only heightened my doubts.
The masala tea I assumed was a welcoming gesture
For typhoid pathogens to enter the vulnerable system.

A wobbling and oscillating roller coaster ride
Is all I could dream of on the morning of the journey.
And to enter that station congested with throngs
Meant donating cell phones and wads to "charity."

The seats, as hard and pointy as stone,
Would leave my back and bones in aching sores.
No "bhaiya" to carry my luggage for half a mile,
No air hostess serving sparkling juice with a radiant smile.

But my experience surprisingly disproved these stereotypes.
The omelette reminded me of Grandpa's fond cooking.
The ride smoothly made on without jolt or jerk,
And the snug seats reclined up to obtuse angles.

Watching the emulsion on the lucid lake
Of scattered clouds diffusing the orange ball,
And ubiquitous shrubbery and coconut palms—
Well, it's elusive to find, isn't it?

And the benevolent passengers at the platform,
Who witnessed my ignominious act of lifting my suitcase,
Gave me a hand instead of breaking into fits.
Oh, how glad I was to be mistaken!

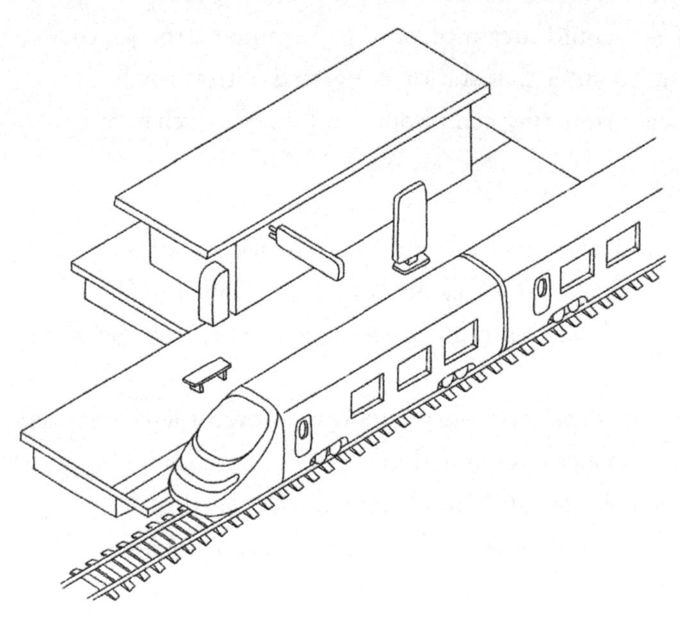

Arsham Hirani

When they're sad to leave a place they've wished to leave their whole life

Expelling tears of grief from their watery eyes,
Even the brave men with their hysterical sighs,
For it is in their so-called second home (school) their last day,
Before, like fleeting fledgelings, they will make away.

Quite ironic, don't you think this puzzling sight?
Where once they'd rack their brains with all their might,
Only at ingenious excuses, they were bright.
"Oh, acute cold and wrist pain, hence I cannot write."
Anything to avert seven tormenting hours seemed right.

Well, these are the reasons for their radical change:
One last mortifying dance as a whole batch,
One last day before friends are made from scratch,
One last day of looting the rich kid's food,
One last opportunity to ruin a teacher's mood.

One last lacklustre "Gooood Mawwwning, Miss Shah."
One last football game where their knees we scar,
One last futile chance to pursue the dazzling star,
One last chance to mock the nerd they've hated so far.

Arsham Hirani

Witnessing my favourite festival, except that I was not a part of it

As the sun pours into the streets, leaping out of bed,
Just a morsel of milk and a rasher of bread.
For water guns, buckets, balloons scrambling ahead,
These unruly mischief makers, away they fled.

To be blotched in a powder of blue and red,
Reverberating cries of ecstasy widespread.
The amplitude, can it be said?
Like unruly animals in the garden, they sped.

Peering through the window in disdain,
Are grumpy old ladies awoken, crying "INSANE!"
Admonishing the revelling children in vain,
Threatening to complain to senior authorities,
If silence and hushed voices, they do not maintain.

Hurling water balloons, buckets repeatedly depleted,
The hilarious moment! The sweeper greeted,
With a bucket of ice-cold water; for his services treated,
Muttering mild abuses, his lividness deep-seated;
"Another year!" they wished the calendar could be cheated.

Arsham Hirani

The most stressful night of a student's life

In boundless volumes, I'm seen immersed,
Notes and books across the bed dispersed.
With apprehension at culmination; I'm cursed
By those bewildering formulas and facts, the worst!
While pivotal concepts before the mirror rehearsed,
To accomplish perfectionism indeed coerced.

Banking on each precious moment before
My volatile memory is washed ashore,
I wash my droopy eyes so that they're awake till four!
While grumpy mother tells me to stay awake no more,
And with iron fists, she pounds on my door.
Well, you might just fail, her wotds I do ignore.

In desperation, I gaze at the ruthless clock,
The time constraint leaves me in shock.
With a book, frantically up and down I walk,
Gallons of strong black coffee in stock.
My vivid memories of the past flock,
And in my jovial heart, they dock.

Of picnics and parties, and frolic and fun,
For weeks and months, there have been none.
After the turmoil and hardships begun,
And lessons proliferated a ton,
Of which a small fraction is surely undone,
Now hoping that the fierce battle is won.

Arsham Hirani

Just another day in an accident hotspot city

One horrid afternoon on a blocked road,
Smirking, the passersby strode.
The chauffeur's fury amused them all,
With police and traffic into a brawl.

A petty accident interrupted the ride,
Against a food van, a car did collide.
The eggs inside spilled onto the ground,
Broken egg shells and yolk were all around.

The BMC summoned to clean this mess,
Everyone appalled by people's carelessness.
The bewildered police stood helpless,
The scene, nothing but a chaotic movie, endless.

"I have a meeting to attend," one cried,
"I have a funeral to attend for my wife just died."
"I have a flight to catch and I will be late."
Three men shouted for there was a longer await.

The traffic forestalled for almost an hour,
Throwing at the police faces of lour.
The cleaners would have to figure out how,
To penetrate this congested mess right now.

Arsham Hirani

My version of a real adventure

No more entrapped in a bustling city and crud,
We now darted through intertwined tracks of mud.
Often erratic on the cragged ground—THUD!
Tracing the magnificent creature beloved.

Binoculars slung on my neck await,
To magnify my vision of the leopard's gait.
This exuberance rests on fortune's fate,
The boisterous lot, the tour guide does berate.

Paw marks printed across the forest floor,
A couple of hundred metres away or more.
A ravenous leopard relishing deer, unmitigated gore!
At last, witnessing the moment we spent a few
thousand rupees for.

For the little cub, the empress preserves the rest,
Who devours every morsel of flesh with zest.
Then tenderly licks its mother appressed,
For this gracious sight, feeling unrestrainedly blessed.

This vast, intruding multitude intimidates and threatens,
The human bait and vulnerability beckons.
The leopard's blatant glare at us deadens,
And flashes its razor-sharp teeth at us for seconds.

It abruptly lunges for our jeep, livid,
"Drive! Our lives in danger," emitted.
Aghast at this abrupt hostility, everyone's timid,
Her swift gait, the screams and shouts in memory printed.

Well, I found this encounter humorous! Odd,
While the leopard chasing for kilometres roared.
Children bawling, women screeching onboard,
The attacker gave up the pursuit, they said, "Praise the lord!"

Arsham Hirani

To all my cat haters, Happy Reading!

Our priceless cat named 'Mylo',
Derived from the phrase 'My love',
Is amiable and nowhere low,
Unlike the 'horrid cat' you know.

Brighter than the nerdy child you grew,
No less loyal than a dog,
Not one squirrel he won't pursue,
Not an ounce of milk he won't hog.

Always up to mischief,
Playing a game of hide-and-seek,
Finding him is not brief,
Do be warned of his cheek.

Though a lot of money,
You're never alone in his company,
Or ever in low spirits,
A best friend and the biggest merit.

Arsham Hirani

Something we busy people need!

Leisurely waves mopping sand,
Reverberating melodies of the band.
Rejuvenating beverages in hand,
The atmosphere fabricated grand.
Unparalleled views of the erratic sea,
Exuberant twilight's mix can be.
Bobbing vessels on the horizon of infinity,
Petty gulls pecking scanty grains in flee.
Mellow gusts of serenity,
Coconut palms in dancing spree.
On sprawling grass, cookies, and tea,
Propelling the football in athletic glee.
Napping on circular rings afloat,
Twining backwaters through a boat.
Teeming with seashells, the tote.

In Shakespeare's 'Merchant Of Venice,' the one who dazzled the most
magnificent countess was the one who preferred the bronze casket over the gold

Intertwining roads of brick,
Bordered by shrubbery thick,
Illuminated by sunlight quick,
Presenting dangling berries slick.

Optimism, for exit in sight,
And sweet chirping through the night.
Maple leaves, fragrant flowers might
Diminish the ominous smell of fright.

Another bewildering track of mud,
With scanty patches of grass spud.
Desolate, barren, saline flood,
Of stony waste, such crud.

Darkness as canopies sunbathed,
And stumps of trees by felling scathed.
The cawing of crows, in mind, engraved,
Distanced from this path, a conclusion is made.

The foot is set on an adorned path,
While destiny unveils its wrath.
Exited the path, none hath,
For dire was the aftermath.

Appearance entrapped the wisest of all,
Success, prosperity did forestall.
In the latter, safety did befall,
Wasteland was the bridge to haul.

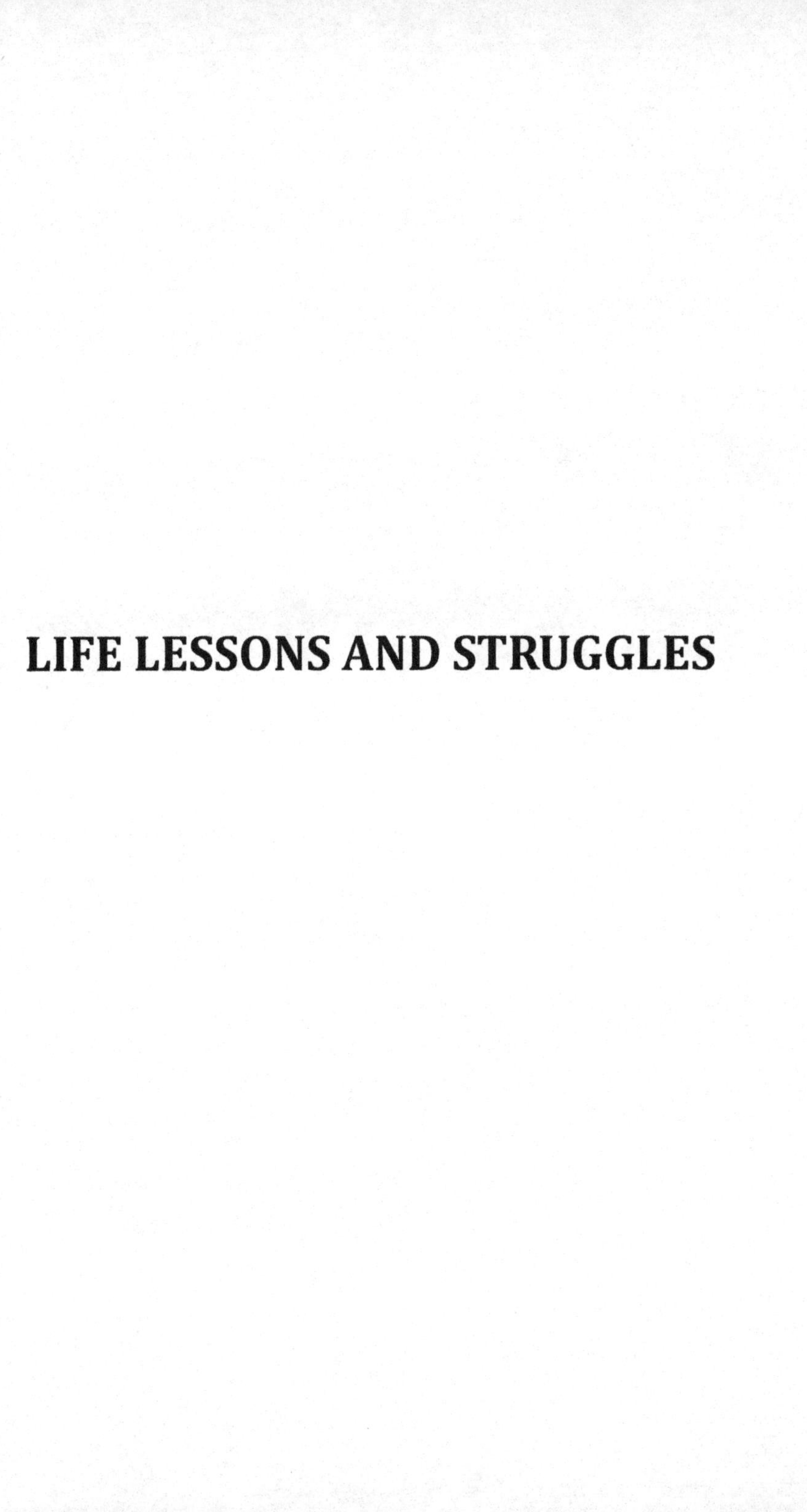

LIFE LESSONS AND STRUGGLES

Arsham Hirani

Human flaw: falling for gaudy appearances

Undoubtedly, the glossy mangoes steal our eyes
Unequalled to the masses surmounted beside,
And blind us to the countless options in sight.
Compelled and incentivized to pick up none other,
In a split second, snatched from the basket,
Unbothered to review nor search it through.

Deceived by the colorful sprays that conceal
The harsh reality of this lustrous fruit,
Only when tested by the sensitive palate,
Does the truth and indecisiveness come to light.
Contradicting its looks, not only chewy but sour,
Who knows the silent harm done?

The only satisfaction was brought to our eyes
Expending time and energy-a worthless waste.
Irreparable vinegar feelings sink into our hearts,
Our hopes of delight quashed.
Those mutual benefits cannot be reaped,
Says time, the authentic teller of the truth.

Surprising as it sounds, but few other men
Who picked those slightly slushed and stark,
As poor in appearance but as rich at heart,
Their seeds planting a bond in their hearts
With vibrant flavours and tenderness and softness.
And now say for yourselves, who's the victorious one?

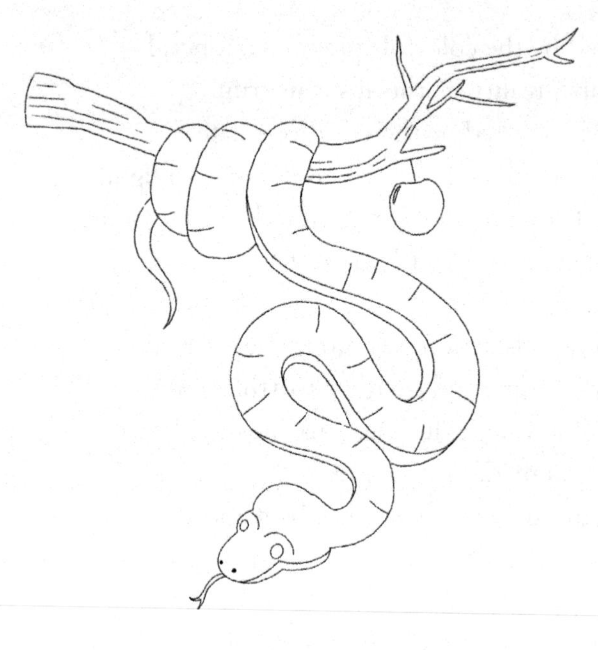

Well, being a jack of all trades can sometimes mean being a master of none

The winsome girl robed in the most entrancing dresses,
Whose exuberance and splendour stole all eyes
And captivated the hearts of these superficial men,
Was a nucleus closely examined at a microscopic level,
Always exhibiting extraordinary properties.

But at the same time at school, studying apt,
Achieving escalating heights of academic success,
Shepherding a reading club of youthful lads,
Entrenching complex vocabulary into their narrow minds;
Marvelling at how she does both, well there's more!

Reputed for being an athlete at the national level,
Would rise the earliest in the morning
And circle the track for hours on end,
Then made to perform some strenuous exercises,
Accounting for an overflowing wardrobe of medals.

However, one day she could do it no more
And crumbled to the intensifying pressure
Of each of these draining and demanding responsibilities;
Suddenly people scoffed at the notion of her glamour
And contended her dressing style was distasteful.

Men would no longer pause and gape awestruck,
Her grades plummeted to historical lows;
She would often frantically ponder for reforms.

Her prestigious position, sabotaged by a competitor.
How she would sob at the nostalgic sight
Of the children listening intently and tranquilly.

Distressed by perturbing thoughts at night,
She no longer had the strength and motivation
To get on her feet and run the track.
Dejected, her dreams were dashed in the dirt
And soon she gave up this pursuit too!

Arsham Hirani

Some people just don't fit into the scheme of things, and
they're perhaps not meant to

Amidst the lush groves in desperate flee,
Where not a single human stands,
From throngs, chatter and boisterousness free,
Preferring to stand on nature's hands,
Called eccentric for being solitary,
Reverberates within, while heaped before wetlands.

Involuntarily partaking in the euphonious singing,
Humming on the beat with the vibrant chirping,
The priceless gift nature's orchestra is bringing,
Which cannot be reaped in the world unrewarding,
Then embraced the trees, sighed, and said,
"We're two lost souls in an environment rapidly changing ahead."

Then with ecstatic cries with the wind, he raced
Upon these merry banks with daffodils laced,
Hurling stones that slide across the water in haste;
His grimy feet in cleansing waters, he placed
Like minuscule fish which waded and retraced;
In this bustling world, he felt irrelevant and misplaced.

Shrubbery intermittently dotted with dew,
Caused by the bleak and cold atmosphere,
Like the tears seldom shed at challenges life threw,
Caused only by the cold world he knew.

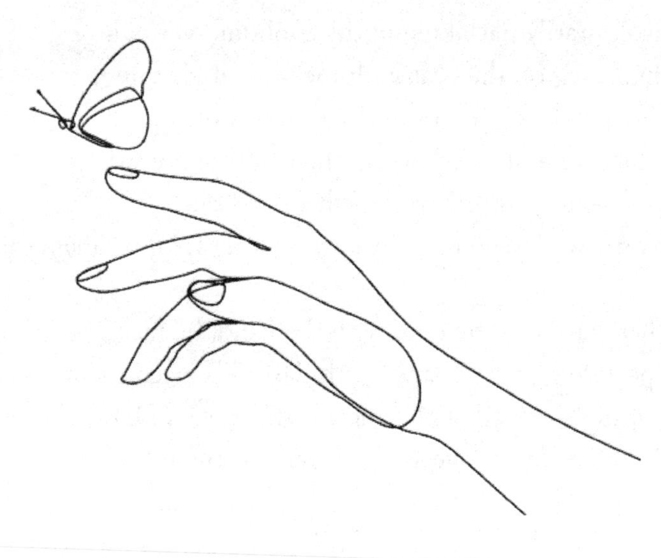

In society, you're either categorised as a star or a mere shadow

A golden decoration in shine
With striking divine,
The star of the tree
in tension free,
catching the eye
of the passer-by.

But another lustreless,
In inferior suppress
At the back of the tree,
With no visibility,
Is always still
Amidst words of shrill.

A golden decoration in shine
With metallic fine,
On a branch quite long,
In a cheerful song,
With the silver one,
Its pair is well done.

While in great brine
On the sideline
The lonely one
In a corner shun,
'Tis disproportionately big,
Thus ignored and hid.

Sometimes you just need to hit that pause

Why not, amidst your strenuous day-
Though crammed with clamouring clients,
Harrowing calculus tests, social sprees, and what not-
Take a deep breath and intently examine your pulse?
Close your eyes and block your thoughts,
And maintain this meditative stance for five priceless minutes,
Which we would otherwise spend scrolling frivolously
Or drift perturbed in the countless concerns of life.

Why not do the most simplest and basic things
Which we so often neglect, procrastinate,
And deprioritise to do these countless "imperative" tasks,
Often forgotten in the hubbub of daily events?
Like holding the door for the frail old woman,
Greeting your teacher with a vigorous "Good morning,"
Expressing simple forms of gratitude to those it is owed,
Or checking in on your dear distant relative.

Why, when whining about boredom and isolation
Saying, "There's nothing happening around,"
Do we not gaze at the million things taking place
That escape the perception of our careless eyes?
Be it the candyfloss clouds in gentle motion,
Or the impoverished vendor packing fruits on the road,
Or routine commuters hopping upon transport-
If only we could take a slight step back!

There's always this proportion: the very few who excel in something, the bulk
that manage to hit the boundary, and the very few who just fail at that thing
no matter what they do——they do get it bad!

Gliding, soaring, manoeuvering in waft
Despite mist, fog, frosty showers aloft,
With loops and turns and bends and curves,
It stoops towards the ferns.

Encapsulated in its ominous claws,
Lie two squirming creatures of flaws;
Such pearls of perfection win applause
From the flock that drops its jaws.

The remaining herd in less remarkable flight,
Saves itself from awful plight.
Though, linearly at a lower height,
It captures prey with conventional might.

But the crippled one with defective wings,
With colossal struggle above it springs,
No prey but ignominy it brings
And falls amidst the spiteful stings.

Can you relate to being trapped in a vicious loop you cannot break?

Those euphoric imaginations containing no bounds,
Leaping from boulder to boulder, train to ground.
Long strides on buoyant whirls of air,
Omnipotence and invulnerability all that we feel.
One's senses appeased to the apex of emotion.
This second world, how enticing it feels to be free!

Yearning for its permanence, as soon one must transfer
Through the portal exiting this fictitious world.
To soon rehash the same and recross the threshold of reality,
First gravitating and then coming crashing down.
The aftermath in the realm of reality must be endured,
However, worth the transitory hedonism.

Exonerating from one's actions on the pretext of circumstance,
Neglecting the truth, one's welfare is predisposed.
Yet how one wishes he could channel his inner strength,
His ethical values proliferate his guilt,
In order to shatter this loop, this vicious cycle,
Into a million shards at his feet of sobriety.

While you feel a person is at his apex, he's rather at his lowest

Behind that animated face and radiant smile,
Those uncurtailed fits of laughter,
Those comedic jokes and brutal slander,
Those rhythmic movements of unearthed authenticity,
Those shrill notes that fear no shame
Was the most aloof and desolate man to ever live.

Whose weeping and wailing knew no bounds,
A man whose company awed, demanded by many,
Felt he was neglected and condemned in hushed voices,
Felt that among the vast multitude with whom
He cherished priceless memories,
Not a single well-wisher or companion stood.

A man who thought he was always guaranteed help
Because of the smiles he never failed to spread,
But when he endured a period of unfortunate circumstances,
Much to his chagrin, the vast multitude actually fled.

Breaths of placidity aloft,
Vexation and tension we do exhaust.
From hardships an interval at hand,
Whose rebellion makes us feel too grand.

Breaths of bravery aloft,
Whose sootiness is felt oft.
In the heart, where irreversible scarring done,
Is transitory adoration and amity won.

Breaths of imprudence aloft,
To prove bravery but by fault.
Well for now, eyes may peep in awe,
But in the future, one inevitably regrets this flaw.

Breaths of disobedience aloft,
While words of wisdom are scoffed.
Secrecy and dishonesty in play,
Until revealed on doomsday.

WORLD ISSUES AND EVENTS

I'm sure even the most hard-hearted will feel an ounce of pity

Out glide the notes from the wooden flute,
Vibrant in nature, soft in sound,
Contradictory to the 'mellow' sounds,
Weaponry and artillery, the root.

Through the city, he plays alone,
Using the remaining gifted hand,
As he trots through lashing rain,
Of rubble and heavy stone.

They sigh, "A break from the explosions acute,"
And gently free themselves
From heaps of concrete above,
As they pause to hear the flute.

The cats into the open sky,
Springing from sordid corners.
Our peaceful friends who have left
Their pile of twigs, fly high.

The flautist plays to the walls splashed red,
And the blazing buildings, towering high,
To honour the invisible dead,
Who bid the earth goodbye.

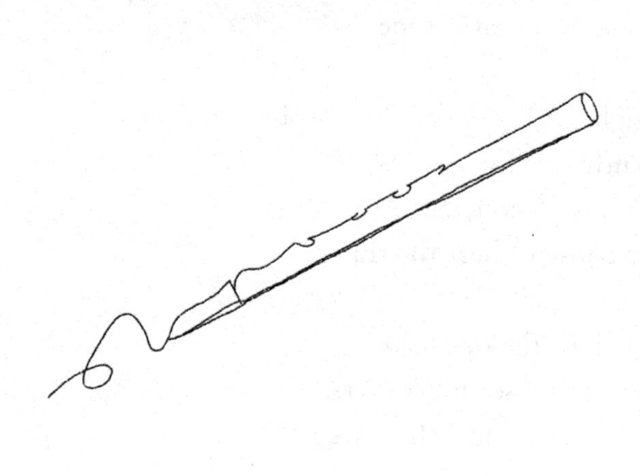

*Can you compare the birds and cattle to a certain group of people under a
pressing circumstance? Take a guess*

In doom the frantic seagulls fly
While averting streaks of bolt.
The sooty nimbostratus enrobing the sky,
Are no bar to the birds that jolt.

Eastward bound through the 'Black Sea',
A cyanide sea of murk,
Is the only gate to vitality
From the sinister threats that lurk.

Blinded by the blanket of mist
And by the wanton winds swerved,
The birds in deep doom amidst
Are shrouded by the fog unnerved.

Capitulated to fate are the cattle,
As territory lost is swifter than
The farewell words in conscience rattle,
That reverberate through the faultless clan.

*What would be your response to a situation like this-one so frequent we've
surely encountered*

With weak limbs, an aged man
Begs for water in his empty can.
Responded by echoes where began,
His skin burning like a blazing pan.
Under sweltering rays that cracked the ground,
Capable of depleting groundwater all around.

On melted, murky, sticky tar
Heaped under an umbrella,
His vigorous fanning is no bar
To the oppressive weather of the hour.

At constant velocity, a car AC
Halts by the pale man to see.
"Multitudes shall pass by him,
 Not my duty, away we flee."
Yet with optimism of 'freedom' complete,
Patiently awaits aid at his seat.

Just when life for the "blue lotus" was starting to get better but slipped away,
things went back to square one just two years ago

With petals lucid blue,
The lotus battles through
The tempestuous gusts which blew,
Often crushed by downpours anew.

Brutal bolts of lightning,
Turbulent waters frightening,
Probability of peril tightening,
Unparalleled beauty whitening.

Barely floating on shallow water,
While averting insect slaughter,
Who knows the next moment at the altar,
Terror will never cease to haunt her.

Rooted to a spot and movement curtailed,
Prosperity and welfare: a promise long failed.
Botanical features were never unveiled,
Rather tender leaves wilt, afraid.

Which problem can you relate this metaphorical poem to? Isn't the current response and plausible outcome most realistically explained?

Away through the night, the skylark sings
An emphatic tune of wisdom.
While the majority sleep it through,
The minor do review.

Away through the night, the skylark sings
An eerie, foreboding tune.
Suspenseful of what the future does behold,
The unfolding of which remains untold.

Away through the night, the skylark sings
A tune against life's justice.
A boon for lumbering men life lay,
A bane for species who reached doomsday.

Away through the night, the skylark sings
A distressed tune of plea.
Out of sight are the children she sang to,
And for her vanished home, to a stump it grew.

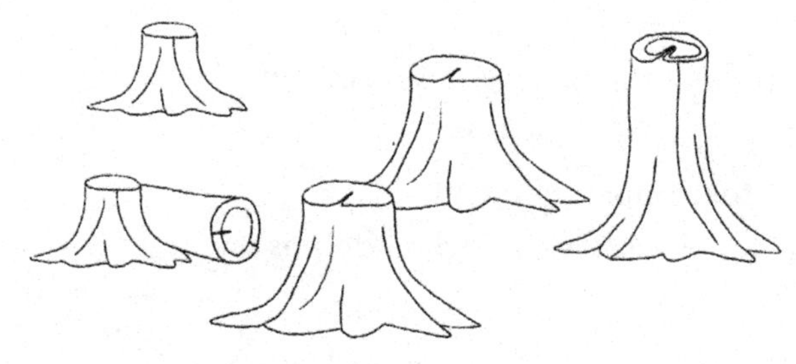

Like a scene from the movies...

Daunting pillars of sand ascend,
The timid child, fear exacerbating,
And dark shadows dull the youthful face
Of vigorous and youth blooming.

With futile attempts to scale the sand,
His feet plunge into such hostile carpets.
And sting his vulnerable skin red,
Tumbling to where the mount commenced.

Anguish and dismay tweaking his malleable mind,
The air of optimism deliquescent over unforgiving sands.
Sand grains of dejection encase his body,
Now suddenly thirst spurs him to free from the heaps.

And with iron-determined feet, he breaks
The adhesion between his murky feet and the sand.
Eying the apex, quite narrow for many,
He begins his next ascent.

United we stand

Like hiving bees, the multitude
Swarm the 'majestic' tower pursued.
Hoisting red banners of rectitude,
Reverberating chants of platitude.

Commanding authority, men in black,
Make futile attempts to send them back.
Admonishing treachery and attack,
The adamant crowd, no bravery does it lack.

Sooty streets now smeared in red,
Yet they resist with no dread.
It cannot be said what was shed,
Many plummeted near death.

POW! BOOM! POW! BOOM!
Shatters, cries, sobs, doom,
But for an exception, there's room
Back to the rampage we resume.

An immediate target now approached,
An elderly woman now reproached
With brutal strikes disdainfully encroached,
Defends her youth, like an animal poached.

Her aged bones withstand no more,
With a feeble cry collapsing to the floor.

Her infant sobbing, "What is this for?"
His rough heart shaken forevermore.
Fainting to the ground at this gore,
His muffled words, "...reach hell's door."

Arsham Hirani

Keep them away!

Tens of thousands of miles away
From conventional civilisation of today,
Penetrated into the forests, one may say,
In the lopsided caves, someone stays.
Blobs of blood glimmer in day
And night, the remanence of its prey.
Carcasses and mouldering flesh lay,
While future victims near doomsday.
His razor-sharp teeth and agonising grin,
And ovoid yellow eyes, one's mind will spin.
A ten-foot-long shadow wherein
His insatiable jaws will slash your skin
And guzzle blood from bodies so thin.
Then leave the flesh to his twin,
Thousands of bodies are his win.
Strewn across the cave they have been,
And stack upon pillars of sin
Their presence, a mystery forever hidden.

Or so the innocent girl accepted,
While slurping her cereal and cold milk,
In front of the television screen,
On the sofa beside her mesmerised brother,
Chills running through her pale skin,
As she wondered, "What if in the silence,
In the deep, dark, black night,

While everyone was oblivious in sound sleep,
He forced open the futile doors,
And grabbed her and took her away."
"Mhmm," said the mother, fobbing her off,
Too preoccupied ordering more stale milk.

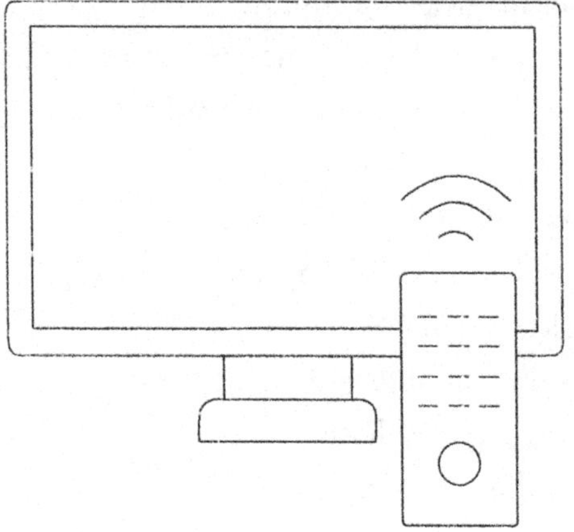

*To the minorities who suffer and struggle to be heard, I'm sure you can
relate to this metaphorical piece*

An authoritative farmer says,
"Yes" to the cows before the gate,
Deaf to the harmless camel that brays,
Who wishes for treatment like the cows as great.

After grave contemplation inside the farm
Unwilling to share, a wall of hay
Is built by the cows, but they struggle
With moral harm for days.

While the cows are excessively fed
And may roam the farm all day,
The camel bound with a rope to his head
Is stuck in the wall of hay.

Despite the cows' words of spite,
The subdued camel bears this plight.
For his righteous voice is lumbered,
By the tyrannous cows, outnumbered.

IndiePress

The best route your story can take.

To publish your own book, contact us.

We publish poetry collections, short story collections, novellas and novels.

contact@http://indiepress.in/

Instagram- indie_press